2006

·1

Letters from Campus

Letters from Campus

COLLEGE GIRLS' INSIGHTS
FOR HIGH SCHOOL GRADUATES

Donna Margaret Greene

New Hope Publishers

Birmingham, Alabama

New Hope® Publishers
P. O. Box 12065
Birmingham, AL 35202-2065
www.newhopepubl.com

Library of Congress Cataloging-in-Publication Data
Letters from campus : college girls' insights for high school graduates / [compiled] by Donna Margaret Greene.
p. cm.
ISBN 1-56309-756-7
1. Women college students-Religious life. 2. Christian college students-Religious life. 3. Women college students-Correspondence.
4. Christian college students-Correspondence. I. Greene, Donna
Margaret, 1947-
BV4551.3.L48 2003
248.8'34—dc21

                                                    2002155134

Cover design by Righteous Planet Design, Inc.
Franklin, Tennessee

ISBN: 1-56309-756-7

N034114 • 0403 • 12M1

Dedication

Laura Celeste Raburn (1964–1988)
Mary Susan Lewis (1969–1993)
Carleton Benners Parnell (1980–2002)

Table of contents

Acknowledgments

I want to thank the more than 3,000 young women who have been and continue to be a part of Community Ministry for Girls. You have blessed me with who you are as we've shared countless adventures together for more than thirty years. You have been blessed to be a blessing to all you come in contact with. Thank you for sharing your thoughts, your hearts, your very lives with me. May our Lord Jesus Christ be glorified in you now and forever.

> "I *have no greater joy than to hear that my children are walking in the truth.*" —3 John 4

Julie and Jim Stephens have afforded me the opportunity to compile and reflect on these letters. I've walked down memory lane as I've sat on their sofa, fire roaring, pen and paper in hand, with a beautiful panoramic view of the ocean and sky before me. It's winter, very cold, and rainy. But my heart is warm, cozy, and full of sunshine. Thank you for the retreat at your Villa Crest.

Introduction

For 30 years I taught Bible study to more than 3,000 girls. Many began coming weekly while in the fifth grade and continued being a part of the program until their senior year of high school. More than 3,000 girls have participated in this "sisterhood" and have built friendships and a network of relationships that will follow them all of their lives.

When they went to college, the girls would leave physically, but their heart ties remained. I received letters from many of them telling of their struggles and adventures. These college girls would send advice for me to give the high school girls in my Bible study, advice to help them prepare for campus life.

Thus "senior advice" was born. It wasn't a planned thing. As girls left home, they remembered various hints, tips, and encouragement from those who had gone before them, and they were now eager to share with those younger girls what they themselves were learning firsthand. Thus Thursday nights, as the high school seniors gathered for their weekly Bible Study discipleship, I would carefully open each letter and read the words of those now-much-wiser girls. Many weeks, there were so many letters that I would read for an hour. The high school girls listened motionless while I read.

I have to admit—I gave the letter-writers a little extra incentive. After I received long, handwritten letters (mostly written on theme paper and many written during class), the college girls received pound cakes in shoeboxes from me as a reward for their efforts.

I have saved these letters since 1982. While straightening up my files, I began to reopen many and found some consistent themes. Because I was looking backwards, I could see what the girls had become and the effect their relationships had had on one another. The letters from college girls encouraged, excited, challenged, and warned the high schoolers coming behind them. Through these letters, the older girls were mentors to the younger. They were one or two steps ahead.

This book represents thoughts and advice given by many girls through the years. I did not use names, except in rare cases. The quoted material presented is excerpted directly from the letters written by the girls whose names are listed in the back of this book. Most letters were written to be read openly, but a few were written to me personally. In all cases I have obtained written permission from the girls to share their thoughts. Three of the girls who wrote letters have since gone to be with the Lord—their mothers gave permission for their daughters' letters to be used. If only I could seek those girls' advice now! It would be perfect.

These are girls who have studied the Bible for a great portion of their young lives. I believe that most are Christians, although only God truly knows the hearts of men (or girls). The girls' backgrounds are from many different Christian denominations. The letters written were mainly from freshmen girls in college. That's the time when advice is so eagerly shared. Yet all four years are represented. The girls attended many colleges and universities, and they are also listed in the back.

Times change. Truth does not. It is my hope that this priceless anthology of thoughts and advice will continue to bless and challenge high school girls through the years as they contemplate college—another of life's great adventures.

And I pray that these letters will remind the girls who have heard senior advice throughout their high school years, many of whom are now grown with daughters of their own, of their youth, their heritage, their process of becoming who they are today.

"Don't let anyone look down on you because you are young, but set an example for the believers in speech, in life, in love, in faith and in purity." —1 Timothy 4:12

Making the Most of the Days

CHAPTER ONE

Making the Most of the Days

"Teach us to number our days aright, that we may gain a heart of wisdom."—Psalm 90:12

Why is it our human nature to often miss the moment at hand because we're looking toward the future or reliving the past? Our lives are not a dress rehearsal. We're each given only one opportunity in which to invest our lives for all eternity or wastefully spend the time entrusted to us. We can't *really* relive the past, and none of us is promised tomorrow. We only have *today*. High school is a once-in-a-lifetime opportunity, and yet our hopes and plans for college often dim those priceless high school days. As you enjoy your last summer before college, live with enthusiasm one day at a time!

Don't spend your time worrying

Well, I must say that starting college is the hardest fun thing I have ever done. Do not spend your last summer before college worrying or planning out your freshman year. Just remember Psalm 143:8: "For I have put my trust in you. Show me the way I should go." I would almost be willing to spend a month in jail just to go back on senior trips or spend one day with everyone all together. Take all the pictures you can now, because sometimes those pictures of my friends from high school are what have gotten me through the early days here at college.

—*Freshman*

Appreciate life as it happens

Hey girls, whatever high school you're from, I'm pretty sure I know what is going through your minds right now. You've watched every grade before you leave, and now it's your turn. You're sick of the college questions, and you've talked it to death with your parents, friends, and college counselors. At this point you just want to get there and experience all of the new freedom and fun times you have heard so much about.

However, during my first year of college I've realized how important it is to appreciate life as it happens. I can remember many times when I was not living my high school life to its fullest, and it saddens me because I can never have that time back. I remember feeling that especially toward the end of the year—dissatisfaction with life. The yearning for college was always the dominant conversation at the lunch table. I know it's easy to just float through the day and not really think about just how many blessings you have all around you, but I advise you to enjoy it while you still can, so you won't look back and regret not investing in every minute.

—*Freshman*

Keep your friendships strong

Tell those girls not to take for granted Bible Study or their senior year. Tell them that it will be one they will always remember. Encourage them to stay right with the Lord. Make sure they keep their friendships strong— even though you may go to different colleges, you can still stay close.

—*Sophomore*

You can't go back

Tell your seniors to enjoy their last days of high school, because once it's gone, it's gone, and they can't go back to it. I feel like I have grown up so much since I've been at college. I have to make all my own decisions and deal with the consequences. I never knew how easy it was to waste time until I got here. Many times I'll find myself talking in someone else's room when I should be studying, but so far I've kept my grades up.

—*Freshman*

No friends like high school friends

Enjoy the time you have with your high school friends. You will not have friends exactly like these again. This is a good thing, though, as diversity allows you to become a well-rounded person. You learn the lifestyles of others and use their positive traits in your own life.

—Sophomore

Carpe diem

The lesson that I have learned after nearly a year of college and want to share with your girls is *carpe diem*, which is Latin for "seize the day." There are so many things that I wish I had said and done and not taken for granted. I wish I had told more people what they mean to me, tried harder to reach out and touch more lives, appreciated the little things that are only noticed once they are gone. I wish I had not been so close to my friends that it kept me from forming new friendships. I wish I had given my mom more hugs and thanked her for all she does for me, spent more time with my brother, and learned how to play golf with my dad. We cannot go back, so we must make the most of what is to come.

I hope that all your girls hear this letter and reflect on their lives and the changes they would make if they knew they were leaving home tomorrow. I understand that high school is a time of uncertainty—we aren't sure who we are, where we are going, or what we believe. For that very reason, it is important that we *seize the day* and snatch every opportunity to touch other lives, because that chance may not come again.

Our lives and time are precious. I wish I had truly seized every day. I urge your girls to dig deep inside and find the courage to be the people they are called to be, living their lives as Christ would want rather than the way their peers dictate.

—*Freshman*

CHAPTER TWO

Preparing for College

Preparing for College

"Finally, [sisters], whatever is true, whatever is noble, whatever is right, whatever is pure, whatever is lovely, whatever is admirable—if anything is excellent or praiseworthy—think about such things. Whatever you have learned or received or heard from me, or seen in me—put it into practice."
—Philippians 4:8–9

The time has come to leave high school behind. Much preparation is given to buying supplies, decorating the dorm room, finding the right roommate—not to mention the right college. Sheets and towels are labeled or monogrammed. You proudly begin displaying your university colors. There's so much flurry and activity, and then—reality hits. You're on your way. Life as you've known it for so long is officially over. You're on your own! What are your dreams, your goals, your aspirations? How much time have you spent preparing your heart and mind? Don't wait till the last moment to prepare. Lessons of life are not best when learned as a crash course.

Creating a new normal

I never fully realized what it would mean to be away at college. During high school college seemed so distant, but as the time grew nearer, my friends chose schools, and before I knew it people were leaving! At the beginning of college I was frustrated—high school was so much fun and so wonderful to me. I loved my friends at home, and I didn't understand why it's such a big deal in our culture to go to college away from your lifelong friends.

Now that I am here, I realize that things will be as wonderful as everyone tells you college is, even though I miss not only my friends but many other things—high school lifestyle in general. This is such a transition! I really didn't know what I was jumping into. I was okay leaving my friends and home and thought everything would be so easy. I just had no idea how strange it is being away from everything you are used to. It's like you go from "normal" (your everyday routine—living in your hometown—going home to your family every night) to having to create a new normal where home is a different place and going to your parents' house is a weekend getaway. It's scary because what you are living now you'll never have again! But that's okay because it's just growing up—branching out and learning how to change and adapt to new surroundings.

—*Freshman*

Trust God

No matter what happens during the college search, trust God and His amazing plan for your life. Cherish every single moment you have with your family and friends (especially your friends in Christ), girls.

—Freshman

Seniors, start praying now!

Well, I'm in heaven. This place is wonderful. God has really blessed me in so many ways since I've been here. He put me in the sorority of my choice and immediately surrounded me with so many Christian pledge sisters who are constantly encouraging me. It's incredible the way God prepared me for college. I prayed all my senior year of high school—seniors, start praying right now! If you focus on God and put Him first in your life, God will do whatever He has to do to prepare you.

—Freshman

Get ready to study

Seniors, start praying now for your future roommates and friends at school. Even if you don't have to study hard to get good grades in high school, get ready—you will in college. It's rough, but tons of fun.

—Freshman

Learn to turn to Christ

My university is very difficult academically. In high school I had to study, but it was not so difficult that I felt I absolutely needed Christ to help me in my school work at all times. Now, I've finally realized that Christ is the only way for me to get by, not only school-wise, but in all aspects of life here in college. One thing that is hard to handle is finding God's answers through His Word in my struggles with classes. To be more prepared for college I think I would have turned to Christ in all situations of high school, even those that might seem easy for me to handle alone.

—*Freshman*

Having a roommate

Well, so far I've survived the first couple of weeks of college! It's strange because I was prepared to be totally *un*prepared for everything, and it has not been that bad. (If that makes any sense at all!) My roommate and I get along great. It's kind of an adjustment having someone in my room all the time and sharing a bathroom with many, many other girls, but it's fun also.

—*Freshman*

Choosing a college

So far college is everything I expected and more. God is so evident here. I went to my first Fellowship of Christian Athletes meeting this week, and it felt so good to worship. The Christian college I'm attending is so different from the big schools where my friends are—it's all right if you don't drink at parties or don't sleep with a guy. It seems a lot easier to be a Christian. I am so happy here and know that God has an awesome plan for my life and that He is really going to use me to impact the campus. I know school is just starting, but I am so excited to see what the Lord puts in my path. Tell the seniors to pray about their college decision and not to worry about it. God will put you where He wants you. You will know where to go.

—Freshman

Don't worry

Donna, I remember that in our Bible study, you read us letters from former Bible study girls who were in college—and now I'm one of them! I know a lot of the high school girls must be starting to choose their colleges. Please encourage them to trust God completely with all of it, because He knows exactly where each of them is supposed to be. I did a lot of pointless worrying, and I don't want them to do the same thing. If we are seeking, He will lead us to His will.

—Freshman

Let it be your decision

I want to offer a bit of reassurance to your lives. Some of you might have pressure from your parents, older brothers and sisters, or even peers as to where you should go to college. Let it be your decision. Realize that the Lord is on your side and will hold your hand as you make your choice and will continue to be near as you journey through life. Have faith in your Father on the road ahead. He knows what He is doing.

—Sophomore

CHAPTER THREE

Adjusting to College

CHAPTER THREE

Adjusting to College

"I can do everything through him who gives me strength."
—Philippians 4:13

College, in a word, is change. A new phase of life is beginning, and this calls for a continuous series of adjustments. You will be stretched, pushed, pulled, and changed. Some absolutes are necessary in a world of uncertainty and relativism. But adaptation and alteration are necessary in order to become a well-adjusted college student. Seeking security or identity only in that which is familiar negates openness to flexibility, innovation, and creativity. Holding fast to absolute truth while allowing room for the unexpected and unpredictable helps turn change into a wonderful adventure.

Free time!

College is definitely a huge change from high school. I think the biggest adjustment for me, besides being away from my family, has been dealing with the amount of free time. I only go to classes for three hours a day, and then I have the rest of the day to do whatever. It is hard to focus on what I *have* to do as opposed to what I *want* to do.

—Freshman

A schedule

Things are just so different that it's hard to have a schedule! It's amazing what I can do on my own. I never realized how much I depended on people! I also realized how important it is that I stay focused on God. Without Him right now, there is no telling how I would be. This is a rough place to be if you are not a Christian.

—Freshman

A home-cooked meal

College is such a big change from high school. I'm meeting a lot of nice people, though. I never realized how nice it was to have a kitchen until I didn't have one. So many times I want a home-cooked meal, and our microwave just doesn't get the job done. I guess there are bigger problems in the world than my lack of vegetables.

—Freshman

People and time

I can't believe I'm writing you my first letter from college! College is good. I already feel like I've been here for a year. I really do. College life is so different from what I expected. I'm amazed at how much I've learned about people. To sum up college, I'd say it's about getting along with people and learning to manage your time. Through those things you can't help but learn so much about yourself. I feel like I have grown up a lot since I've been here. I find that I must always be so aware and cautious of everything. It's a scary world. I'm realizing I'm in the real world now. The only way to survive is to know who you are and what you believe. So many things I have learned in the past really make a lot of sense now. (Oh, I called you one night "collect" but didn't get you. I was having a homesick tragedy.)

—*Freshman*

No slackers here

As expected, I was so nervous coming up here, but I really didn't have any trouble getting acclimated. It has really shown me how precise and purposeful God is. I mean, I got here and spent about the first couple of hours homesick, and then God literally put five of the cutest girls in my path. Ever since, I've been very good friends with them and have never felt out of place. I cannot imagine myself at another school. Just walking around campus I still get so excited that I'm finally here and loving every minute. The school climate is so much different from high school. So many times last year I was tempted to just blow off school work because it just wasn't a priority, but that is definitely not the case here. After class is over, about noon, I head to the library and study until four or five. It seems like such a long time, but it doesn't feel like it because everyone does it. I mean, there are no slackers here.

—*Freshman*

Lots of distractions

In college there is always something to do. Distraction is impossible to get away from, even at the library. It is not only distracting doing your school work, but even getting ready to go out takes twice as long because everyone walks in your room, or you have a twenty-minute conversation with someone in the bathroom, or you have to help everyone else pick out their outfits. It is always tempting to talk and catch up or meet some-one because you don't want to miss out on anything. Stop that temptation right away, because you have to have some sense of self and direction in your life or you will just float right back home. When you have stuff to do, the dorm is the worst place in the world to be, but when you are full of free time—it's the best!

—*Freshman*

Prepare for some bumps

College is not anything like I thought it would be. It's tough, no matter how perfect your school is for you. I think a lot of people expect a perfect transition and are unprepared for the possibility that it may not be an immediate and smooth change. During this first year, I have watched so many people get upset, transfer, and waste part of the best times in their lives because college was not what they thought it would be. Every day is a challenge, whether it's in academics or in social life or other activities. Going to college is one of the best things I've done but also one of the scariest. Every aspect of it has been hard. There's the challenge of doing well in classes that do not even compare to high school, making friends, and making the most of all the money you are spending on your education.

—*Freshman*

Blank slate

When you arrive at college, you are a blank slate to all these new people. At home, everyone knows who you are. They know your parents; they know what you looked like when you were ten. Suddenly you arrive at this new place with a group of strangers, and you can be whoever you want to be. My roommate responded to this new-found freedom by dyeing her hair green. It was great to realize that I didn't want to be different than I had been growing up—that I wanted to continue to be the same person I had been in high school—only more exposed to the exciting adventures in life.

You'll always have to deal with an element of the unknown in a new situation, but if you just keep your head and stay alert, you'll be okay. If the situation gets out of hand, trust in God to get you through. As long as you remember who you are and what you believe in, you'll get back to safety.

One of the best things I did at college was to get involved in a campus ministry and a good church. Being so far from home, I needed a way to feel connected to the values I grew up with. The campus ministry gave me a way to make friends, and they planned all kinds of fun activities. I was able to be involved in a Bible study all four years with most of the same girls. We got so close to each other. It helped me to know there were girls praying for me about tests, projects, peer pressure, and dates. We held each other accountable. The people in the campus ministry became like my family. One time my car wouldn't start at my apartment, and I had to get on campus to take a test. I was sick with the flu and in tears. My daddy always helped me with stuff like that. I called one of the guys involved in the campus ministry, and he came and jump-started the car for me. He even offered to drive me to the campus for my test.

—*Senior*

CHAPTER FOUR

Putting God First

Putting God First

"But seek first his kingdom and his righteousness, and all
these things will be given to you as well."
—Matthew 6:33

In life, one thing is certain: Nothing stays the same. Just
when we feel most comfortable, here comes change. God
designed it that way. He doesn't want us to become too
complacent and secure in ourselves or circumstances; He
wants us to trust in Him. Life is full of choices and possibil-
ities. Some are poor or even bad. Many more are good. But
very few are best. God wants to give us His very best. And
this best comes to those who leave the choices up to Him.
If we seek first His kingdom and His righteousness, all that
we need will be supplied by our heavenly Father, who knows
what we need even before we ask Him. The key is relationship. In order to seek Him, we must know and spend time
with Him. He must be our first priority. In a world of constant change, He remains the same.

31

Don't leave without Him

Well, this time I am the one writing the "senior advice" letter. Weird! This college is truly my kind of place. God knew I would love it, and that is why He placed me here. He has "been my strength every morning and my salvation in time of distress." That is the first thing I pray each morning. With all of the schoolwork, the staying up late at night, the party situations, etc., I have learned that I must depend upon Him. I do not know how in the world I could make it without Him. There is no way I could! God is using so many circumstances and situations to teach me more about Him—to be dependent upon Him. He is molding me more and more into His image. I haven't even been too homesick because, for one, I am so busy, and two, I wake up with excitement each day to see what God has in store for me. Tell the seniors not to leave for college without the Lord: He will guide them and give them perseverance.

—*Freshman*

It's easy to get caught up

Here is my advice. Take nothing for granted. Don't get too wrapped up in yourself, and in things that are unimportant. The things of the world are so appealing that it's easy to be blinded to all that is beautiful and true. It's so easy to get caught up in boys, looks, parties, and everything else. All this isn't wrong, and it's fun! But fun lasts for moments; joy is constant. Enjoy life. Enjoy God. Don't let yourself get distracted from spending time with Him. God is really the only constant wonderful thing in my life.

—*Sophomore*

Fix your eyes on Christ

College is wonderful. I love the people here, my classes, and the Christian atmosphere. I am so thankful to be able to be at this college and am seeing more each day why God has led me here. I am learning that only God can fulfill me. There are so many things going on around me and so much busyness, but I can only be satisfied when I keep my eyes on Jesus.

I have adopted Hebrews 12:1–3 as my theme verses for the year, for it is my prayer that I will strive every day to fix my eyes on Christ, the Author and Perfecter of my faith. I am also learning to depend on God. Although everything around me is changing, God is the same always. He is my one constant. I see that developing one's prayer life and relationship with Christ is the most important thing an individual can do.

I followed your advice and wrote down my standards before going to school. I also wrote down my purposes in life as a Christian. Encourage the seniors to enjoy the time they have together and to truly work to keep each other accountable.

—*Freshman*

Daily time in the Word

God has blessed me abundantly being here—living among such precious Christian friends and participating in lots of great ministries. I have learned much from the Lord about prayer and genuine Christ-like love. My daily times with Him are truly the fuel for the day. Please emphasize to your girls the greatest importance of daily time in the Word and in prayer. Also, being involved in discipleship during high school and college is vital for growth and encouraging others in the faith. I am also learning how essential prayer is.

—Senior

God provides for my needs

I am having a great time at school. Well, the school part is not that great, but the rest is. God allowed me to quickly get involved in some great Christian fellowship through a group here on campus. I am learning how much God really loves me and wants the best for my life. He provides for all my needs if I only seek Him first.

—Freshman

Wait and be still

Over the holidays I got my life back on track with God. I can attribute my contentment here to Him. It is amazing what He has done for me in the short period of two weeks. I feel at peace inside, and things are falling into place. Right now, I am trying daily to make a pure place for God to dwell in my heart. I am trying to cut out the things in my life that do not honor God. I have been studying Lamentations, and it says to "wait and be still." I am also praying for God to be on the tablet of my heart at all times. There is such hope in my heart.

—*Junior*

I just got mad at God

I have been frustrated for a long time with my spiritual walk. Frustrated because I wanted to be like so many great Christians I know. I tried to have quiet times like they had, but it never seemed to work for me. I felt like maybe I just wasn't one of the people that God wanted to be close to. Toward the end of summer I just got mad at God. I felt that He had gone against His Word, and if I couldn't trust Him once, I could never trust Him again. So I started trying to find myself. I was somewhat convinced that you had brainwashed me through Bible Study. I had a tendency to take everything anyone ever said as truth, without checking it out for myself. I put people on pedestals rather than Jesus.

Anyway, I searched for myself in the party scene. I have tried to find my self-worth by the clothes I wear, the people I am friends with, or the boys that I wanted to date. Okay, I said "wanted to" because I never did. Anyway—I didn't find myself there.

Recently I heard a Christian speaker say, "If you are trying to find yourself, stop looking. Go to God and ask

Him who He wants you to be." I asked God to please be in charge of my life completely and not just partially—completely, in that I would depend on Him for all my needs. Please pray that God will give me strength, endurance, and a complete dependence on Him.

—*Junior*

God came with me to college

I am very happy, content, and challenged. God, as He promised, came along with me to college. He hasn't and won't leave me or forsake me. Prayer and Scripture are the two things that I must do daily (at least) to stay grounded. I have to be God's just one day at a time. He is teaching me about patience and His timing. He puts me into many positions where I can share my faith. It has been amazing. I must remember to stand tall and firm on the rock of salvation, because storms and waves will come against me and crash. But God is the almighty fortress, and I am protected.

—*Freshman*

Learning trust

Trust is something that you will completely learn in college. Not trust in a best friend, who will tell everyone about that secret that you didn't want anyone to know. Or trust in a boyfriend, who hurts you so many times, often unintentionally. Instead you will learn true trust in the Lord. He is the only one who will never change, and

He is the only one who will never move. If the distance between you and the Lord has grown, you can be assured that your movement is the reason, and it is never too late to turn and start walking back to His side. What a lovely friend we can find in the Lord if we only look directly to Him with all our troubles.

—*Freshman*

Seek God first

"Seek ye first." This is what God tells us to do. If we seek Him first, then we can trust Him to take care of everything else—everything. This notion is something that I have to remind myself of daily. Life seems to present me with stressful situations daily. I often find myself caught up in worry. However, God offers us a better way to live. He promises to take control of everything if we will only seek Him first.

I might be classified as a perfectionist. I am very motivated and have chosen a challenging path in life. I have found that the only way I receive a sense of peace is if I focus on God and leave everything in His hands. This peace is what leads to a life of true joy. When you give all control to God, you can be confident that you will lead a meaningful and exciting life. This decision to give God control requires trust and is not easy. It is a decision I must make minute by minute. However, once I do, life becomes so much more fulfilling, and I find myself achieving much more. My advice is to seek God first and all else is sure to follow. God has so much to offer us, if we can just choose to follow Him.

—*Junior*

Finding quiet time

Finding quiet time is so important. At first I didn't even know how. My brain was scattered everywhere with new things, and the thought hadn't even crossed my mind until I was actually alone and I realized how much my mind and body craved down time. Whether it is going walking by yourself, to a coffee shop by yourself, on a car drive, or to the library, being alone and evaluating yourself is essential in reaping good things. I feel so refreshed and centered once I have had time to think and pray in an atmosphere without people.

—*Freshman*

CHAPTER FIVE

Depending on God

Depending on God

"And my God will meet all your needs according to his glorious riches in Christ Jesus." —Philippians 4:19

Change can be a scary thing. Many times we don't know what to expect. I've learned throughout life to expect the unexpected. God has given us a roadmap, the Bible. If we follow its guidance, our lives will be peaceful and orderly. If we get off the path, His Word shows us how to get back going the right direction. We must apply God's truths to ourselves personally. This requires dependence upon the Father. We must draw near to Him, trust in and rely upon Him. The more dependent we are upon Jesus, the more security we will have. Interruptions in our routine become opportunities. And those opportunities give way to even greater adventures.

Independently dependent

I am so glad God brought me here, but I am still getting adjusted to college life! I was so content and comfortable in high school with my family and friends. I would do it all over again if I could. But I know I need to get out of my comfort zone to grow. I pray that I can become more independently dependent on God. I have found a pretty spot under a tree where I like to have my quiet times. It's neat.

—*Freshman*

Just out of habit

I encourage all of you to really work on making your relationship right with Christ and strong as possible. It is important to have your whole life under Christ's control before college. That way, when you're making the hard transition to a new school, you don't have to worry about fitting God in—He fits in naturally, out of your own free will, just out of habit.

—*Freshman*

When classes are hard

I'm probably going through my toughest semester ever. I'm taking five senior-level classes, one in French that demands a 7–9 page paper every week, not to mention regular homework. Classes have always been tough here, but they are at an unheard-of level this semester.

No longer am I studying extra hard to make As. I'm studying all the time just to finish work. I don't mean to be down in this letter, because never have I felt so confident of God's plan for me. Quiet times are fruitful and fellowship with others is amazing. I feel like I carry on a continual dialogue with God throughout the day, honestly relating my feelings.

—Senior

I broke up with my boyfriend

Things are well here. I love my house with a front porch and a swing. I broke up with my boyfriend. He is wonderful, but something is missing. But I am content and excited to be fulfilled by Christ alone. That is what I hope for and struggle with. I have realized loneliness does more than help me know my need for Christ; it also helps me find a connection to Him.

—Senior

College is so different

College is going to be a great experience, I know—but starting out has been so new that I have had to rely on God for comfort and support all the time. It really is so different from anything you can think of. I was expecting a "camp" type feeling, but it's not even that because you're not gone for a few weeks. It is truly the end of your life at home.

—Freshman

A firm basis for college

This is the first letter I've written to anyone since I came to college. Anyway, I just remember how special senior advice was to me last year, so I wanted to write and tell you what's been going on. I love school. The first two weeks were kind of hard and lonely because I felt like I didn't have any close friends. It was so cool because God totally showed me that I can't rely on friends and circumstances for my happiness. In fact, the night that I had been praying about how alone I felt, my devotion began with this statement: "The second negative to be controlled is to realize we depend on people, places, things, and events for emotional stability. Jesus Christ is the only one who is able to meet our need for love, joy, comfort, and peace." Isn't that awesome? God was totally speaking to me. One bit of advice I have for the seniors now is to get yourself straight with God before you go off to school. You need such a firm basis for college because life is so busy here that it can be easy to leave God on the side of the road while you try to move ahead.

—*Freshman*

Easy to get on the wrong track

Tell those seniors that I said "Hey'" and that they really need to grow closer to God before they go to college. It is so incredible to be close to God in college because He

44

works so much out for you. If I did not have Him, my life would be terrible because college can be seriously tough and things can get out of hand. I have seen how easy it is to get on the wrong track because there are all types of people here who can bring you down.

—*Freshman*

I panic for a few seconds

My school is so full of Christian people and ministries. It is wonderful! The only thing, though, that has kept me going is knowing that God is with me. Every now and then I realize that I'm away from home, on my own, and then I panic for a few seconds, before realizing that God is right there beside me and will never leave me. That is such a comfort. I really don't know how people do it without Him. I know that I would be home right now if I didn't have the hope and comfort of His presence.

Quiet times are so hard to sit down and do because there are no quiet places and everything is so busy. But I'm really afraid to go through any day without Him. It's so weird, but quiet times are my first priority as far as what I want to get done for the day, but they are also my biggest struggle.

—*Freshman*

Not difficult to lean on Christ

I remember the letters we heard last year from college girls. They spoke about establishing a good relationship with Christ and knowing where we stand with our standards. I just want to let them know that those things are definitely wonderful things to do, but I assure them that it is not that difficult to lean on Christ at this time. We are going through so much with rush, new routines, and school. I think I've become stronger and haven't had to remind myself to pray. I also feel a little bit more of a responsibility to stand out and stand up for Christ. Please pray that I will have courage and strength and wisdom to be able to spread God's Word and answer anyone's questions. I pray that I can make a difference and be the best friend I can be to everyone.

—*Freshman*

Hands open

This has been a great semester. I have learned a lot and I am kind of ready for the year to end. God has for sure carried me the whole way, and I am still in amazement over all He can do. Donna, I remember you always using the example of your hands and how we have to approach God with them completely open. Since I have done that, it is amazing to see all He has taught me and blessed in my life.

—*Junior*

Depending on God abroad

I really came to know the meaning of dependence on God when I made the decision to study abroad for the spring semester of my junior year of college. Ever since I was in 8th grade I had always wanted to study abroad to pursue my second language as well as develop a greater sense of self and the world.

As the time came closer to send in the application and finalize my decision, I experienced some apprehension and doubt. I began praying consistently over the decision and asked the Lord to reveal to me if this was indeed His plan for me. I was confused as to why something I had wanted to do so long was suddenly becoming a huge question mark. I felt in my heart that the best thing to do was to carry on, as planned, with my decision. The dependence didn't stop there.

The journey over to Europe was exciting, yet with each passing preparation day, I realized how much of my comfort zone was going to be stripped away. On the plane ride over, I thought about all the aspects of my life that would soon be different: living with a family I had never met, eating different food, being in the minority with my religious beliefs, and most of all, battling the language barrier. It was at that moment I learned what it meant to be solely dependent on God in everything. I prayed and wrote in my journal and asked that He might calm my fears and allow me to embrace the unfamiliarity. As I began to depend on Him completely, I began to develop a new perspective on life.

Little did I know what the Lord had in store.

The family I lived with was an amazing Christian

family, the food was so surprisingly good that I gained about 15 pounds, I found an awesome non-denominational English-speaking church, and I developed a love for the Spanish language and culture beyond what I would ever have imagined.

The Lord is good. He wants nothing but His very best for His children. All He asks is that we depend on Him, and the rest is just "details," just a part of His plan . . . .

I know from experience.

—*Junior*

CHAPTER SIX

Leaving Home

Leaving Home

> "But we have this treasure in jars of clay to show that this
> all-surpassing power is from God and not from us.
> We are hard pressed on every side, but not crushed;
> perplexed, but not in despair;
> persecuted, but not abandoned;
> struck down but not destroyed."
> —2 Corinthians 4:7–9

Everyone is homesick at sometime or another. At college, you may experience homesickness at many times—often when you least expect it. Home is where the heart is, and if Jesus Christ is at home in your heart, you're never away from home. Circumstances and feelings may dictate differently, but the reality is—you're never alone.

I missed my friends so much

I never dreamed college would be so tough! The school-work is not difficult, but emotionally it is hard. I have always been a strong person. I can only remember crying two, maybe three times when I was in high school. I think I cried every night the second week I was here. The first week was fun, and I loved it. But the second week, when things calmed down, I started to miss my friends and the comfort of home. I've made a lot of friends here, and I know a lot of people, but it's not the same. None of my close friends came here. I've never been homesick in my life, but I just missed my friends so much! I was also having trouble with my roommate. We are very different. Anyway, I am thankful because God really taught me to depend on Him! I am learning a lot in my quiet times. They refresh me and are the only thing that is comfortable and familiar here. It is beginning to feel like home. Thank you for teaching me the importance of having a set time for quiet times.

—*Freshman*

First day of college

I came to college yesterday, and it was awful! I wanted to just go back home with my family. It was the most emotional strain I have ever felt. My mom was so upset, and my dad started to cry for the first time ever! My brother almost cried. I was praying and asking God to calm my heart and help me know that this is what I am supposed to do and that He has great plans for me here. I fought off the tears and had a good quiet time before I went to bed and woke up feeling great! This is definitely the biggest change of my life, and God and I have become even closer through this.

—Freshman

A sleepover every night

I was excited about going off to college. Believe it or not, I was even looking forward to the freshman dorm. I thought that it would be like a sleepover every night. Mutual friends put me with my roommate, and we had only met twice before we moved in. We got along great, but as far as "a sleepover every night" . . . she had a boyfriend.

At first if she was still out at bedtime, I left the lights on in the dorm room so she could see when she came in. I would wake up the next morning and the lights would still be on and her bed made up, and she'd stroll in wearing her clothes from the night before. A little slow to catch on, I was still doing this in November, you know, just in case she came home. Finally around December, I began turning out the lights and sleeping like a normal person.

Then the phone calls started. You guessed it: her parents called around 7:30 A.M. at least once a week. I would tell them she was in the shower, so asleep I couldn't wake her up, or had headed down the hall for pizza last night and must have slept in another girl's room. After these excuses, I would call her boyfriend's house, they would rush over and walk in the room just as her parents called back. Finally, around April, her dad told me, "We like your stories, but we aren't idiots!" Believe it or not, this is what I learned when I left home freshman year:

1. Sleepovers aren't all they're cracked up to be.
2. Parents know a little more than we think they do.

—*Freshman*

Not "there might be"—there are!

In the fall I go back to college for my second year. I am glad I came home after my first year of college; I needed it. I made so many mistakes this past year, and I needed to be home this summer for several reasons. I had to come home to take a couple of summer school classes. My grades weren't very good this year, and I needed to make up for some of my goofing off. The thing I learned the most this year was that my parents really were right, and not just about a couple of things, but everything!

Mom and Dad were so strict on me in high school, and for good reason, as I can see now that I have finished my freshman year without "the rules." I know that my parents set the rules for my own good. Well, like my parents tried to tell me so many times, there *are* consequences. Not "there might be"—there *are*! I can even hear it now: "These rules are to help you, protect you, not to hurt you," my parents would say. Why didn't I listen? I think I broke all of them; I tried it all, trying to find fulfillment in boyfriends, my sorority, friends, alcohol, and partying. Donna, don't worry—I was not too crazy, but enough that I had a major shift in my priorities. In my mind I kept thinking, "God is going to forgive me, so why does it matter?" Again, my parents taught me there *are* consequences. Not there might be—there *are*, and now I know this.

Donna, I made so many bad choices, and now I have to deal with the consequences and heal. I have opened up more with my parents lately; I am realizing the value of their wisdom. Mom and Dad have told me, beat it into my head even, that God loves me. How many times have I heard that! It was easy for me to take in high school because I pretty much obeyed the rules, because I *had* to. I have begun to learn that I *desire* to obey the rules.

—*Sophomore*

I miss my family

I am wondering why I chose a college that is five hours away from home. The only people who know me here are two girls who went to my high school, and they are sophomores. I miss my family and my dog. The girls on my hall are not like me. They have different values and backgrounds. They are from Florida, Georgia, South

Carolina, North Carolina, and Tennessee. One of them asked me if every one in Alabama likes Moon Pies and RC. They also want to know why people in Alabama are so crazy about football. I am tired of having to meet people. The next time I will go home will be Thanksgiving. I can't wait.

I just got off the phone with my mother. My aunt and uncle are visiting, and the entire family is going out to eat. I am walking to the cafeteria alone because my roommate has gone home for the weekend. I hope I can find someone I know to sit with. One of my friends gave me a cross-stitched Bible verse for graduation that says, "The Lord your God is with you wherever you go" (Joshua 1:9). That is what I am clinging to. I know God is here. He will lead me and provide friends; I am not alone. Please pray that I will find a church. I have no idea where to go. Since I don't have a car, I am going to have to find a ride with someone.

—*Freshman*

There are so many choices

It is a little scary being this far away from home. No one really knows me here. You know I went to school for 13 years with the same group of kids. Most of the teachers knew my brother and some of the teachers knew my parents. Now no one knows anything about me. All of my friends went to Bible Study and my church youth group. We had so much fun together. None of them drank or did drugs, and we all were committed to purity in dating. We supported each other. My parents set boundaries, and they had expectations for me. Now at college, I am responsible for myself. My parents have no idea what time I go to bed. They don't know the new friends I have made. No one makes me get up for church. I can do just about anything I want. There are so many choices about activities to be involved in. My entire hall went to a party last week, and I just did not feel comfortable there. I found two other girls who were ready to leave. I don't think I ever really felt negative peer pressure until now. This is the time when I am going to have to take a stand and get my identity from Christ in me, not my family or friends. Here is a quote I found: "The best way to stand up in the world is to kneel before God."

—*Freshman*

A heart-wrenching goodbye

The transition from high school to college was harder than I had expected. For the rest of my life, I will never forget the heart-wrenching ten-hour drive to college. In a packed Suburban so full that you could not see out the windows, my parents and I made the long trek to begin this new chapter of my life. I cried halfway to school, and fright overwhelmed me. I did not know anyone, had met my roommate once, and did not have my sister there for me, as she was studying abroad. All I could think about was that I should have stayed closer to home and made the easy decision, like all my friends did, to go to school in-state. Being the family person that I am, I had no idea how I would make it on my own so far away, in a place so unfamiliar.

My parents stalled as long as they possibly could, helping me move in and get settled. Then we went out for one last lunch together before I had to begin eating nasty cafeteria food. With the exception of a few words, we were silent. As we drove back to the dorm, my heart pounded. My dad pulled in front of the dorm and looked at me and said, "This is it, buddy." I lost it. I began to cry uncontrollably and did not want to let go of my parents. We all cried together and embraced one last time, and I knew the best thing to do would be to turn around and walk away. It took everything in me not to chase after the car as I watched it drive off in the distance.

—*Freshman*

Far from home

When I was admitted to the university of my choice, I was thrilled but also tentative about this huge change in my life. A true Southern girl, I would be thrown into a diverse melting pot of students from all over the United States and the world. As the opening days of my freshman year loomed ahead, I began to be apprehensive about this drastic life change. Most of my high school friends chose a college close to home, and I envied their ability to be independent but also come home on weekends if they wanted. My parents fully supported any decision I made about school, reminding me that I could always transfer.

Once I set foot on campus, I knew I would not ever want to leave. However, saying goodbye to my parents and watching them leave to drive the 1500 miles back home was a reality check. I had my cell phone and my computer, but voices and e-mail were no substitute for the familiar comforts of home. Looking back almost two years later, I realize that being completely removed from my natural surroundings has helped me to determine who I really am and what I want in life. Leaving home is a difficult step that we must all take sooner or later, but with family support and faith in God, it can prove to be a wonderful thing.

—Sophomore

College as an opportunity to break away

As far back as I can remember, I absolutely despised spending the night out. The problem wasn't the new and unfamiliar place; it was the fact that I would be away from home and not with *my mommy*! I tried camp and it just wasn't for me, and I actually missed out on various opportunities because of my homesickness. But I took college as an opportunity to "break away" from my comfort zone. I left home and attended an out-of-state college and basically left behind all of my security and

59

comfort, but I knew I had to do it for myself. I know that I needed that separation, and going away was the only way I thought I could do it. I could not be happier with the decision I made and know that without removing myself from my comfort zone I would have been cheating myself out of many wonderful experiences.

—*Freshman*

Dealing with Loneliness

CHAPTER SEVEN

Dealing with Loneliness

"For I am convinced that neither death nor life, neither angels nor demons, neither the present nor the future, nor any powers, neither height nor depth, nor anything else in all creation, will be able to separate us from the love that is in Christ Jesus our Lord." —Romans 8:38–39

There's a tremendous difference between being alone and being lonely. A person can be completely alone and not feel lonely at all. On the other hand, a crowded room can be filled with extremely lonely people. Loneliness can make us feel sad and empty. But being alone can fill us up. Ours is a world of chaos, busyness, and constant noise and activity. Yes, Jesus invites us to come away with Him and rest. He invites us to be still and quiet. Confidence and contentment come from being with Him. College can be a time of aloneness at first, but your best Friend is always with you. You are never really alone.

My only friend was Jesus

Life here is so different from anything I ever experienced. The first few weeks were very hard. But I know that the Lord was in control. Without His strength and encouragement, I don't know how I could have managed. More than ever I had to draw near to Him. It seemed strange to say, but for a while my only friend was Jesus. And I know that the Lord sent me that sadness so that I might completely depend on Him. And once I had turned it all over, things began to come together.

—*Freshman*

Have a quiet room

Loneliness . . . yes, I still get lonely, and Christ is the perfect person to turn to. It's great to have a single room where I can drop what I am doing at any time and have total silence, which I spend meditating on God's Word, praying to Him, and listening to Him at the same time.

—*Freshman*

Begin an eternal relationship

Tell the seniors to really get in the habit of talking to God every day. It doesn't have to be a formal devotion, although that is the ultimate aim, but just make Jesus your friend. When I got to school and watched my parents leave and had to walk up to the third floor of my dorm all alone, I don't know what I would have done without Jesus there to comfort me. Being alone is a frightening thing, but if you have a personal relationship and Jesus is your friend, you can't be alone. I made it my goal to make Jesus my "comfort zone." It really does work. Donna, please encourage the girls to go ahead and make the commitment, because if they don't now, they never will in college. You can always say, "Okay, I'll start doing a quiet time when I can manage my own time and don't have anybody telling me to do this or that," but that will never happen. If your relationship with the Lord is not strong before you go to college, it is only going to fall on the wayside. It is sad to say, but there is so much to do that if you don't make time for the Lord, you will never spend time with Him. High school years are the perfect time to begin this eternal relationship. If I didn't have it, I don't know where I would be at this moment.

—*Freshman*

Home a little too long

I have settled back into campus life better than I expected to. Being home was fabulous, but I believe I was home a little too long. I became a little too comfortable, and saying good-bye was not easy. Things are so simple, stable, and secure at home. I long for that feeling here.

—*Sophomore*

I had to force myself to open up

When I left my comfort zone and went to college, I felt a feeling of loneliness in a way I had never felt before. It was a feeling that I would never find anyone to relate to or who could understand me as well as my friends and family back home do. Because of this belief, I would keep all the little things in that were bothering me and shield myself from expressing myself to my peers. As the little things began to build up, I realized I had to force myself to open up to others and ask for their advice and thoughts on the things that were troubling me. In doing this, I began to create more complex relationships and laid the foundation for what are now wonderful trusting, honest, loving, and reliable friendships.

—*Freshman*

You have to want to be happy

The most challenging experience I had was transferring schools the middle of my sophomore year. I had made all Cs my freshman year, money got tight, and I couldn't decide on a major. My parents decided I should change from the small, expensive private school to a state university.

It was so hard for me to understand. I was so happy where I was—part of "the best" sorority on campus, involved in a wonderful new church and discipleship group, nominated for homecoming court. I was into everything. I went camping, hiking, volunteered at a handicapped school, hung out with my friends, and I was growing like a weed spiritually. So what if my grades were Bs and Cs!

Transferring was hard—harder than I anticipated and hard because my stubborn spirit made it that way. I moved into a house with four older girls I didn't know while my friends from high school lived on campus. I had to take core classes with freshmen. I ate lunch most days by myself. I couldn't find a church I liked. My friends had their own friends and forgot about me. Boys didn't ask me out. I didn't drive my car for weeks because I didn't know how to get anywhere. I began to resent my parents for "making" me transfer colleges. I became depressed and thought, "I will never make friends like the ones I had before transferring!" So I didn't try. I was miserable and had never felt so alone.

I don't know how it happened, but one day I realized I had to *desire* to be happy. The saying, "Joy is the deep-seated confidence that God is in control" became my lifeblood. It didn't happen overnight, but eventually I realized I needed to make the effort. I needed to become involved on and off campus. I needed to have people over, introduce myself to people in my classes, meet people in the community, go for long walks. I learned to trust God, not only with my circumstances but despite them.

When I graduated, I had had more than fifteen roommates, served in the student government, worked in a coffee shop, run a marathon, and been a babysitter. I graduated *cum laude* and received the "Most Supportive Student Award" from my school. I had made literally hundreds of friends.

Looking back, I know God was teaching me about obedience and His faithfulness. My advice is to not spend so much time and energy dwelling on circumstances that we cannot change. God is everywhere, in everything. Listen to Him, read His Word, be committed to prayer, and learn to hear His voice. His peace does transcend all understanding. And when we learn to trust and obey, we find true joy. Know that God is in control—despite our circumstances.

—*Senior*

The night of the dance

I miss you and all my friends from home. This is the night of one of the big dances at school. My roommate and suite-mates all have dates, and I am sitting in this dorm room all alone. I just got finished taking pictures of everybody, including several of the girls on my hall with their dates. I may be the only one on the entire hall without a date. That is a depressing thought! Well, I can sit here and feel sorry for myself or I can do something for somebody else. I remember all those pound cakes and cookies I helped you deliver over the years. It seems like you were always doing special things for people. It is true that thinking about somebody else takes your mind off yourself. So I am going to make cookies and notes for some of my friends.

Have you ever made cookies in a dorm kitchen? People started coming out of the woodwork. At first they would just pass through, asking what smelled so good. Then they would stop and talk, and when I started giving the cookies away, we ended up having a party. I am not the only one without a date. One of the girls told me that she has been crying for the last hour because she broke up with the guy she has been dating for two years. She bought a new dress for the dance, had her hair all fixed, and the guy called an hour before the dance and said he wanted to date someone else. They do everything together. She feels rejected and afraid that she will spend all her weekends alone. I gave her a quote from *The Search for Significance*: "I have great worth apart from my performance because Christ gave His life for me and therefore imparted great value to me. I am deeply loved, completely forgiven, fully pleasing, totally accepted and complete in Christ."

I am so glad that I made the choice to come out of my room instead of feeling alone and lonely.

—*Sophomore*

Exchange student mumps

I can still remember my feelings that late July day as I boarded the plane as an exchange student, headed into the unknown. With tears in my eyes, I watched my family and friends wave goodbye through the dark tinted windows in Concourse C. Every emotion known to mankind was pent up inside me, from sadness to excitement to downright fear. I knew not what lay ahead of me.

My new family met me at the airport in Geneva, and they were divine—a little different from the "Swiss Family Robinson" I had been expecting. Even with the language barrier, I could tell that they were phenomenal people.

When we arrived at my new home in the mountains, I hit the sack, only to wake up the next day with the mumps. I wanted my mommy. My cheeks were so swollen that I couldn't do anything. This was by far the loneliest point in my existence. I couldn't talk to anyone, my family was halfway around the world, I couldn't eat, and I couldn't go anywhere.

At this point in time I became closer to God than ever before. He was the only person I could actually talk to. We talked for hours upon hours, and I had never felt so secure. God became my best friend. I realized what an amazing part the Lord played in my life as He turned everything around for me.

Soon the mumps were gone. I made lots of friends, learned French, and brought others closer to God by translating from French to English in my youth group. Even though I started out being lonely, God really taught me a lot about trusting Him and living my life in a godly manner.

—*Freshman*

Not prepared for the loneliness

Throughout my senior year in high school, so many people, including you, Donna, helped to prepare me for college. I was ready to face the drinking, the drugs, the cheating, eating disorders, sororities, dorm life, and just about everything else. I guess the only thing I wasn't told about or prepared for was the loneliness. Or maybe someone did tell me, but from the comfort of a loving home, tight community, and close friends, I couldn't imagine the depths that loneliness could reach. But here I am, nearing the end of my freshman year, and feeling completely alone. Not all of the time—there's not even a pattern to it. It hits me at night before I go to bed, walking to class, or even when I am at a campus ministry meeting, surrounded by hundreds of other people.

While I wasn't directly prepared for the loneliness, in so many ways I have been indirectly prepared. The discipline of one-on-one time with the Lord each day keeps me trusting in Him and looking to Him. This is comforting, but I am not sure I always believe Him. Most people seem like they are always so happy and content, but I guess people say the same about me. Anyway, thank you for constantly reminding me of the importance of building a personal relationship with Christ early on and for reminding me that He has felt everything we feel. It is humbling to think how lonely Christ must have been as He died on the cross and that "neither height, nor depth . . . can separate us from the love which is in Christ."

—*Freshman*

CHAPTER EIGHT

Developing New Friendships

Developing New Friendships

*"There are friends who pretend to be friends, but there is a
friend who sticks closer than a brother."*
—Proverbs 18:24 RSV

Friendship is one of the greatest gifts that God has for us.
Most people genuinely want to have close friends, but
friendships are hard work and take effort on both sides in
order for a true friendship to be formed. Real friendship
takes time. Often we are placed in new situations where we
don't know a single person. College can be such a place.
Seek to find people who are positive, encouraging, and
godly. Lonely times can be a blessing as they draw us to that
one true friend who will never leave us or forsake us. Look
around. Take notice of the people around you. Build bridges
wherever you go. You never know what new friend God may
want to bless you with.

It takes time

It takes time to develop friendships with the people you really care to be around. Don't get discouraged if you don't like your dormitory hall or feel at first like the only friends you will really make are the ones on your hall. You never know who God will place in your life. The loneliest times of your first semester are when you really learn to cling to God and pray fervently.

—*Freshman*

God sent me a bud

One night I was feeling lonely because it was the beginning of school and I didn't know a lot of people. I pulled out my prayer journal and asked God to show me a friend and help me not to feel so lonely. The next day I went into class and met a girl who knew my roommate. We talked, went to lunch, and spent the day together. She told me that the night before she had prayed also because she was talking to one of her friends about how lonely she felt. Her friend told her to pray and she did. Then we met in history class (which we both dropped because it was going to be pretty tough). Now we are buds. We are so much alike, it's crazy. We are on the same page with our walks with God. We're really focusing on putting God in the center. I encourage all the seniors to start now and pray for their roommates, their friends, hall mates, and classmates.

—*Freshman*

Surround yourself with good people

I have learned the importance of the people you surround yourself with. Bible study girls, we are so richly blessed with Christian friends. Thank the Lord for these girls who surround you now, and begin praying for your friends in the future. I started praying for my friends in college at the end of my junior year in high school, and now I am just so thankful that I am surrounded by such uplifting girls. Granted, I still long for my high school friends, and I am not at that deep level with anyone here quite yet, but I know that in due time, the relationships will form and I will be amazed at all God does with my friends.

—*Freshman*

Cultivate girlfriends, not just boyfriends

From my experience of having a roommate who met a guy and has dated him all year since the first week of school, I'd advise entering freshmen to focus more on making friendships with girls, rather than dating a guy seriously during the first semester. My roommate only has four girlfriends—she almost didn't have anybody to room with next year because she has spent so much time with her boyfriend. She has not made the effort to develop friendships with girls, but she will need girlfriends if she ever breaks up with him. She will need friendships in life.

I have another friend who has been dating a guy here since before she came to college, and she makes it a point to split up her time going out with him and going out with the girls so she can be developing both relationships. Seems like a good idea to me.

—*Freshman*

Choose friends carefully

I want you to tell the seniors to choose their friends carefully next year. I definitely think they should keep up with high school friends but also branch out. The people you hang out with could make you fall. It is so hard to be strong as a Christian and to be different from others, especially when you start making friends. The most important thing to remember is that your friends, ultimately, won't be your judge—God will. There are lots of wonderful people in college, but you must look for them.

—*Freshman*

Keep making new friends

Tell the seniors when they get to college not to let themselves reach a stalemate in meeting others after the first month or so. It's easy to do that—but keep reaching out and letting God naturally guide you to make friends because it's such a blessing and support to make new friends.

—*Freshman*

Love one another

Although six of my really good friends enrolled in my university this year, I find it necessary to look to Christ to help me find other friends and also to strengthen my previous relationships. I trust that He will show me who exactly I need to hang out with and put my trust in. "Love one another." That verse constantly runs through my mind in these times of introducing myself to other people, trying to figure out if they are the right friends for me or not.

—*Freshman*

God takes care of me

College life is definitely different from anything I have ever known. When I first arrived here it seemed like everything just slipped into place for me. Everything seemed perfect. It seemed God had provided a group of friends for me that would last forever. After the first couple of months, I started to realize how different it is here and how different these college friends were from those in high school. The kind of bond and closeness we have in my hometown takes a long time to develop. It's hard to realize that you only have a couple of friends in a big school like this who you can really talk to and share with. God is teaching me to depend on Him. He will always provide and care for me. I still sometimes get sad and wish I could be home with all the security of high school, but that is when I realize that God has it all taken care of and I don't have to worry.

—*Freshman*

One great friend

You cannot prepare yourself for leaving your friends. Everyone has that one friend who knows everything about you. You are blessed if you end up at the same school, but if she doesn't, you are also blessed because your friendship will grow stronger in another direction. It is fun to watch your friend grow in another world without you; then you both can share stories about your new lives.

Begin to pray now for everlasting friendships. I have learned that college friendships are different than high school—not that one is better than the other. In college, friends become like family because your family is now away. You need each other in different ways and see each other in different circumstances. I don't think anyone leaves college without at least one great friend. I usually have some sort of connection with the people I meet—friend of a friend, grandparents know each other, travel to the same place, or something. It's funny how God puts those crazy connections in your life with people.

—*Freshman*

Find Christian friends

The best advice I could give to you is to choose your friends right. This applies especially to those who go to schools where they don't know many people. Often when people are new to a place they are vulnerable; they hang out with the first people they meet, and as much as I hate to say it, you are known by the company you keep. So my advice is to pray to God to place holy, Christian friends in your life when you arrive. College is full of temptations and decisions, which is why you have to be strong and make the right choices, because it is so easy to slip up.

—*Freshman*

People who understand your heart

It's really hard, if not impossible, to develop deep and meaningful relationships with people who don't understand your heart. If they don't understand your main motivation and desire in life, which is to live for God and know Him better, they can't truly understand your heart. Freshman year is busy and exciting, and it's easy to get wrapped up in what seem to be the most fun activities and friends. However, all the excitement and newness will fade by senior year, and those friendships can only remain surface deep. Remember to actively seek out a group of Christian friends from the start. Getting involved in a small group girls' Bible study is one of the best ways to find a core group of friends who will support and encourage you in your walk with God.

—*Senior*

CHAPTER NINE

Sorority Rush

Sorority Rush

"Serve one another in love. The entire law is summed up in a single command: 'Love your neighbor as yourself.'"
—*Galatians* 5:13–14

Not every college girl will be interested in rushing a sorority, but social sororities and fraternities are part of the life of most campuses. Many colleges also have service organizations and academic fraternities to which students can belong. But whatever our interests are, we all like to belong. We all like to be chosen. Many times there are disappointments—girls say that sorority rush often consists of the highest highs and the lowest lows. Many girls are elated to receive the bid of their choice. Others are heartbroken and may even drop out of school, feeling dejected and unwanted. But remember, God has a plan for each life, and that plan is perfect. No matter what our dreams and their outcome, God will work it out for His glory and our good if we turn our dreams over to Him.

Sisters in prayer

I am so happy about the sorority I pledged! We went on a sisterhood retreat on bid day, and it was awesome because six of my sisters and I got up thirty minutes before everyone else and went out and prayed together. That was really special to me, and those same girls are all going to have a Bible study together. I am so excited. I have so much opportunity to praise the Lord, and I'm making the most of every one. I spent most of rush on my knees. God is working in my life and I'm so thankful.

—*Freshman*

Second-choice sorority

Tell the girls who are planning to go through sorority rush that if they really commit the whole situation to God and trust Him, then He will definitely put them in the place that is best for them. He does not make any mistakes! I did not get my first choice sorority. But when I walked into the room where all the new pledges were gathering and I saw who was in my pledge class (there were a lot of Christian girls I recognized), I was so pleased to be in my sorority, and I was excited to see God's will unfold.

—*Freshman*

I questioned if sororities were for me

Rush was great for me, and I was treated very nicely, but for some of my friends it was harsh and downright cruel!

My roommate was very hurt a few times throughout the week and then again on bid day. I was excited about receiving a bid, but it was very hard to enjoy because so many of my friends were hurting. It was a mess. So from that point on I was very unsure if sororities were for me at all. Seeing so many hurt people really makes you wonder if you want to be a part of the thing that hurt them. To make a long story short, I decided to stick it out a bit longer and hopefully glorify God in all of it.

—*Freshman*

Sorority candlelight

I love my sorority and feel truly blessed to be a part of such an outstanding group of girls. Today we had a candlelight ceremony for a girl who got engaged—it was the neatest thing! Don't worry, I don't think I'll be having a candlelight anytime soon. I'm enjoying being young, healthy, and carefree as always. But the candlelight inspired me to start a journal to my husband—sort of an accountability in a sense. I think that when I get married I'll get his initials embossed on the journal and give it to him. Good idea, huh?

—*Sophomore*

The wild sorority

Well I made it through rush. What a week! I thought I knew what to expect, but I was wrong. The first day was extremely tiring. I have never met so many new people!

Each day went basically the same but a little better. I ended up pledging a sorority that I didn't think I would choose. I just really loved it and knew that was where God wanted me to be. I really don't know why, because most of the girls are really wild. Maybe God wants me to be a light to some of the girls who don't really know Him. Just please pray that it all works out wonderfully.

—*Freshman*

Two groups of friends

On bid day when I opened that small envelope, I felt as though it held my future's happiness. And it did—just not the future I was expecting. I had been offered a bid from my second-choice sorority. I know it wasn't the end of the world, but it sure felt like it. I tried not to let people see me cry because some girls on my freshman hall had not received a bid from any sorority, much less their second choice.

My friends all had bids from my first choice sorority. I think more than sad or hurt, I felt scared. I was going to spend the next four years with sorority sisters I didn't know. I didn't have a negative impression of them; I didn't know them enough to have much impression at all. I was upset that I was not going to be where it was familiar.

In retrospect, however, I can see that the good has far outweighed the bad. I'm on my own, and I love it. I managed to have the best of both worlds! I kept my same friends from freshman year, even though we pledged different sororities. I live in a house with five members of a sorority not my own. I have an entirely different group of friends who my sorority sisters don't know. My sorority sisters live, eat, sleep, and breathe with each other. I usually eat at my sorority house and go to sorority functions with that group of friends. It is a broadening thing to get out into unfamiliar territory and to make it familiar. You might discover, as I have, that what you thought you wanted may not necessarily be the best thing for you.

—*Junior*

CHAPTER TEN

Setting Standards

Setting Standards

"Do you not know that your body is a temple of the Holy Spirit, who is in you, whom you have received from God? You are not your own; you were bought at a price. Therefore honor God with your body." —1 Corinthians 6:19–20

"Be on your guard; stand firm in the faith; be [women] of courage; be strong. Do everything in love." —1 Corinthians 16:13–14

It takes unusual people to really make a difference in the world—people who are not afraid to be different, to take risks, to stand out from the crowd. They are real human beings with shortcomings like anyone else, yet their lives display excellence even when no one is watching them. As a child, I had a poster in my room that read, "You are what you are in the dark!" That's true character, void of deception or hypocrisy. Authentic, genuine people become heroes. You may be that hero for another person. You may be the one everyone watches. Set your standards high. Don't settle for mediocrity. Make a difference!

Develop strong morals

The other night my roommate asked me if I thought I had good judgment. I thought about it and said, "Usually, yes." She then asked me how I got it. It really made me appreciate all that I was blessed with throughout my growing-up years. I mean, I was taught good judgment at home. I learned to ask God for it every day, and my friends helped each other decipher right from wrong. I was constantly learning when to say yes and when to say no. But here there are so many people who are clueless as to right and wrong. If there is anything I could say to incoming freshmen, or to anyone for that matter, it would be this: develop strong morals.

—*Freshman*

Set your standards

Set your standards up front. I know you have heard that so many times, but it is so true! There are a lot of decisions you are going to have to make in college, especially about drinking, drugs, etc. It is a whole new world here, and people will know and respect you based on the decisions that you make!

—*Freshman*

Surrounded by temptations

Last year we talked a lot about setting standards, but I never realized how important that was until I came to college. Here students are constantly surrounded by temptations, and I am so glad that I had already set my standards. Thank you for encouraging me to do this. Encourage the seniors to do the same.

—*Freshman*

Discipline or regret

The old song declares, "You've got to stand for something, or you'll fall for anything." True success comes from knowing God's will and obeying Him at every turn of life. That means persistence, determination, and commitment to the priorities of life—God's priorities. Standards must be thought through, analyzed, and written down. An excellent life doesn't just happen. Delayed gratification is required. You must choose between the pain of discipline or the pain of regret. How will you hurt?

—*Freshman*

Alcohol abounds

I love college, and I am having a great time. Being here, however, has made me realize how important my walk with the Lord is. At my college, and I'm sure all over college campuses, alcohol abounds. The other night I went to some fraternity parties with some of my new sorority sisters and was so overwhelmed and surprised by the easy access of alcohol. They have free "girl beer" at all parties, which shocked me. All I wanted was a Coke, so

I asked one of the guys who lived there where I could find one, and I had to buy one from the vending machine. I was just amazed that alcohol was free (for minors, too), yet I had to pay for a Coke. I am so happy that I was strong enough to withstand the temptation to drink. Tell all the seniors to set their standards before they step foot on campus because it is so easy to fall here.

—*Freshman*

The "walk of shame"

I absolutely love college, although the work is very hard. My advice to seniors is to set your goals before you ever leave. There are many girls here who are talked about for weeks after they've done the "walk of shame"—after they spent the night in a guy's room. You have to know how you are going to act at parties and toward guys. Not only in social standards, but please set goals academically also. I will definitely be happy to get all Cs here, but that is not my goal. I'm striving to make all As and Bs.

—*Freshman*

My choice about drinking

My choice not to drink since I've been at college has been the biggest blessing. I think it has given me more confidence, and I still have so much fun. Tell any seniors who are wondering what to do about that to decide not to. They will be amazed. I've had so much positive feedback—people saying how they respect it, etc. They're so floored that you can have so much fun without it. Plus it eliminates so much hassle with not worrying all night about getting beer.

—*Freshman*

Actions count more than words

Drinking in college was always such an issue with me. I don't know why, because I never drank in high school and I never intended to drink in college. However, I was always afraid that the temptation would be too great. It is not, girls! I am reminded of the verse in 1 Corinthians that promises us that "God will not allow you to be tempted beyond what you are able, but with the temptation will also make the way of escape, that you may be able to bear it" (10:13). It is possible! My friends and I and so many others enjoy college just as much as everyone else and have chosen not to drink. It's amazing how many witnessing opportunities have risen from that one simple decision. I encourage you to prayerfully consider the choices you are making even now because they will affect your decisions later. And remember that we are fighting the good battle for the Lord, and our actions count more than our words. As Donna always says, "The way you live either crosses out or underlines what you believe!"

—*Freshman*

People respect you for your choices

College is a totally different experience. I have already seen hard-core drinking, and I have only gone to a couple of parties. At the first party, everyone kept asking me if I wanted a beer, and so if you want to avoid that, just carry a cup of water or something. But the most important thing is to start praying about your college experience. Pray for your friends and for your standards. I did and I'm not struggling with it. Grow as much as you can now in your faith, because the closer you are to Him, the stronger you will be. College is a fun time—just remember that people respect you for your choices. I am starting to see that!

—*Freshman*

First impressions can last

I know they know this, but advise the seniors to be cautious about the hook-up scene. All I've seen it do is cause boys to lose interest in the girl. If they are worried that by not hooking up boys won't pursue them, it's totally the opposite. Boys like and respect and go for the respectable girls, while the others get talked about all over campus. Boys talk. Donna, you know how you tell us it takes your life to build your reputation and a second to ruin it? Well, in college you're sort of starting from scratch again, so don't start out on the wrong foot! First impressions can last in college. So know what you believe and stick to it. It's really not hard because God rewards you, helps you, and you end up better! People realize how silly some of the wild college scene is around junior/senior year and calm down. Invest all four years. Don't go too crazy and get a late start.

—Sophomore

God will provide

I am seeing what it is like to hunger for God—time is solitude. I have found a small, secluded room near my dorm room where I can go in the morning to pray, be silent, sing, and read the Bible. I can even gaze out the window at God's beautiful creation. The people here are so neat. God has provided me with some wonderful friends who really keep me accountable and encourage me—what a blessing! I am especially encouraged by the committed guys devoted to seeking the Lord. Tell the Bible Study girls not to lower their standards. God will provide a godly man!

—Junior

An immediate reputation

Over the summer I decided what I was going to do in college and what I wanted to do. I did not want to have an immediate reputation, so I was careful about going out, etc. I have seen some of my new friends get carried away with the whole college scene, like having sex with someone they had met that night or getting so trashed that they vomit to the point of convulsions. They already have a horrible reputation to carry around for four years. It is tough to stay focused, but through making mistakes and experiencing heartache, you find out what is truly important and what you really stand for. I know that each and every one of you has a good head on your shoulders, and I hope that you will have a great freshman year.

—*Freshman*

Don't compromise on sex

Before I came to college I felt I was prepared for everything, that I could face it all myself. I was wrong. Since I have been up here I have been alarmed at everyone's nonchalant attitude about sex. I know very few virgins up here. Because I am a virgin I sometimes feel like the oddball, but I am so proud to be that oddball. Most of my friends know my stand on sex and are very supportive and even are a little envious of what I have. Recently, one of my close friends lost her virginity to her boyfriend, whom she had just broken up with. This bothered me a great deal. I asked her if she regrets her decision not to wait, and she replied, "It's like I don't even care anymore. It's no big deal. Everyone else has done it." Her statement bothers me so much. The point of this letter is that I want you to tell the seniors, do not compromise your stance on sex! When I was in high school this was very easy for me. Sex just didn't seem to be an issue. For whatever reason, I was not ready for what I see here. I am so happy that I am still a virgin and am going to remain one. Not only do I not have to worry about the consequences that come along with premarital sex, but I can also weed out the boys who like me for who I am and not what I can do for them.

—Sophomore

So many influences

I found out that the guy I had a crush on was really wild! I didn't see it at first, but later it became obvious. I learned my lesson. No matter how secure you know you are in a relationship with the Lord, it is amazing how many influences around you will try to weasel their way into your spiritual life. College is a completely different world. I thank the Lord for the foundation of my relationship with Christ. It is the most important thing in life—ever! I realized that before, but until I moved away from family and friends, I never truly understood what is in the world, and how easily a person can be influenced if they do not already believe strongly in God. I see how tons of people are clueless. It is sad. There are so many people who need the Lord and seem so lost without Him—only they don't know it. I only hope and pray that people can see the light through me and I can share my faith.

—Freshman

Accountability partners

I have never met such an encouraging and godly guy. He definitely knows how to treat a lady. We go to church together and pray together. This is the first time I've ever had an accountability partnership with a boy. It is such a wonderful feeling to know that our relationship is centered around our faith.

—*Freshman*

Set your standards before college

I love everything about college life now, but at the beginning I felt alone. My roommate and I got along great, but she did not have the same moral standards as I did, and it was hard to talk to her about certain topics. Also, I was a part of an athletic team of girls who were supposed to be my friends. I went out with them several times, and all of their parties were the same—a lot of alcohol and smoking. These were varsity scholarship athletes, and I could not believe they were such partiers. Girls, college is hard work, and it takes time to adjust. I know you have been told this a thousand times, but it is *so* important to set your moral and spiritual standards *before* getting to college. Don't delay in getting plugged into a Bible study or a Christian group. Also, explore the different churches in the area and find the one that suits you best. And when you feel alone at times (it happens to everyone), just talk to God. He is always there for you, at all times. He has a plan for your life, and sometimes you just have to let Him do the work.

—*Freshman*

Finding your identity

From personal experience I've learned that one of the hardest things, especially during the transition period from high school to college, is the discovery of who I really am. In high school, it made me feel "cool" that the majority of students knew me and the people I hung out with. I didn't realize that everything that I was doing was reflecting on my own character. I am saying that, without realizing it, we place ourselves in situations that make us feel good and wanted. The truth is, with or without this group of friends you are just fine. Through Christ you are strong enough to relate to all sorts of people and stand as an individual.

Acceptance is something we all struggle with in high school. It's important to be seen talking to only the good looking, cool, or even rude people. Well, honestly, these kinds of people burn out. I find it interesting to see people who don't live through Christ who have to continually cover for themselves by trying to act "cool." Finding your identity does not come overnight. It is found through prayer with God and finding peace in His Word. I have not completely found my identity, yet I pray to the Lord that I will live the life He has planned for me. You will be much happier with yourself and your college experience if you find yourself through Christ.

—Sophomore

All the cute boys

Boys, wow, they are everywhere, always and everyday! All the cute boys are overwhelming at first, but sit back and watch them first. Remember that everything always works out; don't ever call them, and just be yourself. Just because a guy likes you and calls you, don't just suddenly change yourself to conform to his ideas. You will be disappointed in the end. Always make sure that he knows where you stand first, otherwise you might find yourself trapped. If you find yourself not liking any of the boys, go to the library and walk all around it because you are more likely to find a good, nice, and smart boy there.

—Freshman

CHAPTER ELEVEN

Eating

CHAPTER ELEVEN

Eating

*"So whether you eat or drink or whatever you do, do it all for the glory of God." —*1 Corinthians 10:31

I was a stewardess for American Airlines in the early 1970s. This was a time when the job was such a privilege and so glamorous. Our appearance was to be impeccable, like that of a model. This was during Twiggy's era. Being thin, extra thin, was of paramount importance. I knew nothing of the words *anorexia* or *bulimia*, but I remember hearing of and meeting girls who looked emaciated. An article later appeared in a women's magazine speaking of this strange phenomenon that was affecting models and stewardesses. The girls were starving themselves.

Today this is rampant. Every college campus is flooded with girls who will not eat or eat too much. It is of epidemic proportions, and girls entering college are at the highest risk for eating disorders. This is a complicated issue to deal with and one all girls will face, whether actively or passively.

My friend has bulimia

Another one of my friends told me last night that she throws up after she eats. I've never been comfortable with the issue of bulimia, because I don't understand it. I wish God would give me some way to understand and help her. Her self-esteem is the issue that started it, but how do you change that? She knows what she's doing is wrong, but she can't get away from the mentality that she would be happier if she lost 20 pounds. She thinks she'd have a boyfriend and everything would be fine, if only . . . . I'm not trying to judge her, but why can't she accept that God has a plan for her and the boyfriend will come when it's right? Why can't she find a comfort in God and turn it around? I hear what she's saying and how "off" her perspective is. Her object is pleasing others, but that's not going to help her get better. I feel so helpless, and I've prayed about it for some time. It saddens my heart to think how many people struggle with this because of our society and what it stresses.

—*Junior*

The "freshman fifteen"

Food is something every freshman is scared of because of the forbidden "freshman fifteen." Supposedly, the typical college freshman gains 15 pounds in the first year. But you don't have to be scared—it's so simple. Eat three meals a day when you are supposed to eat them.

For example, do not eat past 8:30 at night. I don't suggest keeping food in your room if you have a problem with eating late at night. Vary your meals. Don't eat at the same place. Take the stairs if you are feeling fat, but remember you are walking to all of your classes, so you are getting exercise. Also remember that gaining weight and growing is still normal. It is hard at first to adjust to eating differently than you did at home, but you will eventually discover a plan that suits you.

—*Freshman*

A senior's story

I want to describe a struggle of mine that began in college with the hope that my story will prevent even one girl from falling into the same trap.

To this day, I am very concerned when I overhear people talking about how many fat grams are in a hot dog or a candy bar or how many calories are in a Dairy Queen Blizzard. It is amazing to see how fast one's mentality on food can change in the period of one year. For me, it was my freshman year of college. Upon entering, I was a fairly healthy eater, but being exposed to the cafeteria and endless quantities of frozen yogurt, cereal, waffles, etc., combined with a major drop in my level of exercise, resulted in a gain of twenty pounds. As my jeans started to get tighter and my love for food soared, I began to get a little nervous, so I ate, whether I was hungry or not.

I also took an interest in the habits of my roommate. At the time, I did not know that she was struggling with a severe eating disorder. She counted every calorie that entered her mouth, and there weren't many. What's more, she was devoted to 1.5 hours of exercise every day, and boy did she look good, and didn't I long to have her figure? Even when I realized that she thought about food too much and that she was obsessed with exercise, I still longed for her little figure. After all, the boys were calling to ask *her* out.

When I went home for the summer I went with the motivation to lose weight and be disciplined. All summer I exercised 7 days a week, and I felt a tremendous sense of guilt if I missed even one day. I greatly reduced the quantity of my meals and labeled "bad" all foods with more than 5 grams of fat. I would sometimes *allow* myself one dessert a week since I had such a sweet tooth. By November, I had lost 30 pounds. Was that healthy? Probably not. I did not starve or damage my body (we have a gracious God), but my thoughts were taken captive. I was obsessed with diet and exercise.

Exercise became a form of torture. I dreaded it. A good workout according to me was one in which the treadmill told me I had burned over 300 calories and one in which I had managed to use a few more machines such as the bike, the stairmaster, free weights, whatever was available. Food and exercise controlled me, my thoughts, my actions, my mood, my life. I lived from meal to meal. All I thought about during class, walking to and from class, running errands, and studying in the library was what I would eat at the next meal. It didn't matter if I was hungry or not. I would eat what I had pre-determined to be an "acceptable" amount. I was completely self-absorbed, always worried and paranoid. My weight on the scale each morning determined whether or not the day would be a good day or a bad day. If I went up a pound, I wouldn't eat much, and if I lost a pound, I would be extremely happy. And keep in mind, this was a gradual process. I have been told (and I believe) that Satan will wait a lifetime to set you up. He was gradually taking my heart and devoting it to food, exercise, and my appearance. I wanted to stop thinking about food, but I couldn't. It would not leave me alone. It haunted me in the morning, the afternoon, at night, and in my sleep.

This is when God stepped in and provided a chance for me to escape this bondage of food. It happened when I invited one of my most respected, God-loving, Christian friends over to my apartment for one of my delicious layered pies. It consisted of fat-free graham cracker pie crust, a layer of fat-free cream cheese mixed with fat-free milk, another layer of fat-free chocolate pudding, topped off with a layer of Cool Whip (1 fat gram). I was rather proud of my clever invention. After all, I could eat as much as I wanted, because it had no fat! This is when my friend told me of a talk about eating disorders that would be held at the Christian Study Center on campus, given by three Christians who had all suffered from different types of eating disorders and who had all been cured by Jesus Christ.

I went, and I had no idea that she was one of them until she rose to speak. You see, I had put God in a box. He was merely a part of my "Christian/church" life. After all, what did God know about food? Food wasn't His area of expertise. These were the first lies I had to uncover. In the course of several weeks, God taught me many things about food, and, more importantly, about Him. He knew about my temptations, my sweet tooth, and my fear of not fitting into a size 8 pair of pants. He knew of the guilt brought on from finishing a whole dessert by myself. He knew it all! Once I realized God was *there* for me, that He *loved* me, that He *wanted to help* me, that He *carried* His *cross* for me, things started to happen. "Come to me, all you who are weary and burdened, and I will give you rest. Take my yoke upon you and learn from me, for I am gentle and humble in heart, and you will find rest for your souls. For my yoke is easy and my burden is light" (Matthew 11:28–30).

You see, God created our bodies and food. He wants food to be something we enjoy and take delight in, but also something we leave behind once we get up from the dinner table. He created food for when we are hungry. And He created our body with instruments to tell us when we are hungry—for example, a grumbling stomach. If we aren't hungry, we don't need to eat. It's that simple. But how do you stop thinking about it?

There are two verses that have really meant a lot to me. Matthew 6:25 says, "Therefore I tell you, do not worry about your life, what you will eat or drink; or about your body, what you will wear. Is not life more important than food, and the body more important than clothes?" If your mind starts to slip to thoughts of food, meditate on this verse. Write it on your heart. Ask God to take away those thoughts and to fill your heart and mind with love.

The other verse is 1 Corinthians 6:19–20, "Do you not know that your body is a temple of the Holy Spirit, who is in you, whom you have received from God? You are not your own; you were bought at a price. Therefore honor God with your body." That verse really hit me hard. Every time I over-ate, ever time I under-ate, every time I worked my body too hard, I wasn't damaging my body but rather God's temple. My motivation to be skinny, my need to win the compliments of my peers, the approval of my parents, the gaze of college boys, all of these desires were completely self-centered and in no way did they bring glory to God, my Father.

I have learned now, when my thoughts slip to food (which they frequently do), to turn to God. Eating disorders or "disordered eating,"—whatever you choose to call unhealthy eating—are not instantly cured. They take time. It is a long, long healing process, and, without Christ, you may never be healed. One needs to pray and ask God to consume one's thoughts rather than food. It is amazing how this simple change has changed my life. Instead of leaning on myself and my own efforts, I can fall on Christ.

—*Senior*

We all knew about her problem

Eating is one of my favorite pastimes, and I was blessed with a metabolism that allows me to eat freely. I have never had to battle my weight as so many young women do, so I can't speak from personal experience about eating disorders. I can, however, describe how it feels to live with someone who suffers from one.

My roommate has bulimia. She is an insecure girl with an overly controlling mother she tries desperately to please. She tries to look more like her peers, to gain control over her life, and to lose weight the only way she knows how. She has suffered from this disease for more than five years, and the symptoms of malnutrition are evident. Handfuls of hair come out when she showers. She has her period two or three times a year for only three days or so. Her skin and nails are dry and are constantly cracking. Her body is being victimized by her disorder.

They say that the hardest step to take in the direction of recovery is admitting that you have a problem. This she has done, confidentially, on a few rare occasions to some of our roommates. We are all aware of what goes on behind the bathroom door. We all see the hair in the shower. We all witness her bizarre and unhealthy eating habits. Everyone who lives with her finds it impossible to ignore, everyone except the one to whom it is all happening.

Although she refused to go to counseling herself, we sought the help of a counselor because we did not know how to handle the situation. It is frustrating to go out to dinner with someone who orders an entrée and then eats only a few bites. It's annoying to listen to someone complain about being hungry when they have intentionally denied themselves food or have purged what little they have eaten.

This may sound cold and insensitive, but it is hard to live with someone who has a problem and will not help herself. It is still harder to watch someone deny the help she is offered. We cannot force her to seek professional help. All we can do is be patient and supportive. I guess that maybe it is not as cut and dried as it appears on the surface. This is something that she may figure out on her own one day. When she does figure it out, her problem will be much easier for her to face if she has a support group that will be there for her.

The best advice I can give to someone who finds herself in a similar predicament is to be patient and understanding. Eating disorders reflect far more than a mere desire to lose weight. Encourage the person to seek counseling, and if he or she refuses, seek counseling yourself. You will be far better equipped to deal with the circumstances if you can understand the disorder and the effects it has, not only on the person who is directly involved, but also on others who are close to the situation.

—Junior

My struggle with anorexia

I began struggling with anorexia in my junior year of high school; it hasn't gone away. I finally made my way to college after 3 hospitalizations during my senior year of high school, and I just knew that my disease (I call it a disease, not just a disorder) was finally going to disappear; wrong. During the first semester of college my eating disorder was growing stronger. In November, I landed in the cardiac unit of a hospital, at high risk of cardiac arrest. There, I became the patient of an amazing Christian woman who happened to the best pediatric cardiologist in the city; she and I grew extremely close. She reminded me that I was "one of God's sheep." She introduced me to a Bible verse which points out that God provides food for the birds: "Are you not as worthy of nourishment as they?"

I was released after only five days, and life seemed to take an upward turn. I was remarkably healthy over the next few months. After a summer at home, I moved into a sorority house for my sophomore fall semester. Classes were in full swing and I was in church every Sunday morning, but I knew I couldn't continue on the same road much longer. I remember sitting in front of the mirror, crying because I was so frail; I could barely make it up the stairs or to class, and I slept in sweatshirts with a heater on (even during a hot September in the South). No one knew how bad it really was. My mom and brother were planning to visit me in late September, but that fell through after the September 11 attacks; part of me was glad because I didn't want them to see me.

I avoided trips to the doctor, but my mom was persistent. In mid-October, I was "forced" to the health center; Mom said she was flying out that weekend if I didn't go to the doctor. I weighed 68 pounds, was "throwing" numerous PVCs (pre-ventricular contractions), and the doctor wanted to admit me immediately, but I signed an AMA (Against Medical Advice) not realizing what I was doing. I walked out of the Student Health Center that day, scared to death, of death, and feeling lost, alone, and hopeless.

The next Monday I received several messages from the health center doctor; she basically said that I could drop dead at any second. If I didn't respond by 2:30, this doctor was going to call my mother to find me. I got someone to drive me to the hospital, sat in admitting and waited for my doctor. Looking back, I don't know how I managed to listen to everything she told me; God was definitely holding me. I was told that my liver enzymes were so high that my liver might not recover (that would mean a transplant); I was severely anemic, extremely malnourished, and my heart was barely hanging on (my pulse was in the upper 30s—a normal adult rate is between 60 and 100). I had an NG tube inserted in my nose through which I would be fed nutritional supplements 24 hours a day (I would be eating too). In the coming days, I had an ultrasound, echocardiogram, received a transfusion, and had numerous IV fluids. I weighed as little as 60 pounds (50% of my ideal weight). My doctor knew that I needed a miracle to survive. The first night I was in the hospital, I didn't sleep. I was afraid I wouldn't wake up.

The next day my doctor prayed with me as usual, and I could tell that she was scared. I remember telling God that night that I was "ready;" I was tired of living, tired of fighting the disease, tired of causing such stress and experiencing it, tired of spending money on treatment that had led me in circles, tired of feeling like a burden, and tired of losing a battle against Satan. My thoughts were, "If this disease is going to lead me to death, please go ahead and bring me to heaven."

I went to sleep that night, and I awoke the following morning. That was my sign; I believe that was God's answer to my prayer. Heaven wasn't ready for me yet, so I was going to fight this disease. I knew I wasn't alone— God is my strength. The next two weeks in the hospital were filled with visitors, phone calls, medical tests, good reports, bad reports, and important decisions; I decided to enter an inpatient treatment center, something I had been fighting since the beginning of my illness.

In early November, my mom and I arrived at the facility. I was nervous, but the girls and staff were amazing. I met some of the most incredible and inspirational women during my 14-week stay (initially planned to be 3 weeks). I learned so much about myself and my relationship with God and others. I left on Valentine's Day, and I have been back in my hometown since then.

I can't say that the road is easy, but when I am weak, God carries me. As safe as I feel with Him, I am scared because I have no idea what tomorrow will bring. I have to trust Him and have total and complete faith that He is in control; God is the *only* rock in our lives. Family, friends, good days, bad days, health, wishes, and material things; these all come and go. God is an "ever-present help"; He tells us that He will *"never leave us or forsake us."* Think about that—it doesn't get more comforting than to know that the most powerful spirit in this world is *always* with us.

I may struggle with this disease for the rest of my life, but I will fight, knowing that every day I wake up is a gift. As you can see, I will not finish college in the typical four years, I have no definite career plans at this point, and I may never be able to have children (my life in itself is a miracle). But I know that I am always in

God's hands; that, girls, is the safest place to be. I wish you all the best in the road ahead.

—*Sophomore*

Defending Your Faith

CHAPTER TWELVE

Defending Your Faith

"Therefore, my dear [sisters], stand firm. Let nothing move you."—1 Corinthians 15:58a

"All Scripture is God-breathed and is useful for teaching, rebuking, correcting and training in righteousness, so that the [woman] of God may be thoroughly equipped for every good work." —2 Timothy 3:16

A stark realization of college is the fact that not everyone believes like you do. High school tends to be comprised of groups of friends who have similar value systems, beliefs, and interests. At least they tend to be from the same community in most cases. College campuses, however, are seas of diversity. Christians are called to be non-conformists—to swim against the tide. It takes courage to stand alone—especially when the crowd seems so right. And not only are we called to stand but to share with others why we are standing. Know what you believe and be ready to defend it.

I never realized how sheltered I was

I love everything about this place, but sometimes the people scare me. I never realized how sheltered my home community is. My mouth drops with every conversation around here. It's wild. But the good thing is I am still amazed and still the naïve girl I was last year. It has made me stronger, and I have learned not to rely on others for my spiritual life. I do miss the encouragement of home, but I am finding my niche and I think that will come in time. I am so thankful for all the teachings and background I have had. Some people are so lost up here. I often find people in these intellectual debates. Sometimes I wish I knew enough to jump in the conversation, but I tend to just smile to myself. I am just so thankful I know where I stand and where I am headed (or at least God is getting me there).

—*Freshman*

Studying religions

I am so interested in my religion class. It's kind of a comparative look at Eastern vs. Western religion. Right now we are studying Buddhism. It's so neat to see how different my beliefs are from theirs. It seems that Buddhism arose from suffering and has a lot to do with becoming indifferent and passive to life's situations, while Christianity arose from God's love for us and has a lot to do with caring and active interest in living my life for God. Anyhow, I found out today that by letting myself be free from emotions and by realizing that I had no soul I could reach "Nirvana." How cool would that be?! (You know I'm kidding.) But I did think of you, Donna, when the professor told us that we could raise our grade by 10% by meditating like a Buddhist for two weeks. It was like everything I've ever been taught screamed, "No!" Don't worry, I'm taking the grade without points for practicing Buddhism.

—*Freshman*

Religion research paper

Here is a copy of my research paper for religion class. Honestly, Donna, I wrote 1000 words and then deleted it and started over because it was not me writing the paper. Once I stopped trying to write textbook-y technical stuff, I finished it in no time at all. I did have a hard time with a few things, though. I kept saying "us" when I would refer to Christians. That is a big no-no. My professor also would not let us use "Lord" to refer to God and "Jesus" to refer to Christ. Kinda strange? But it is finished—and it is basically what I believe, and if he disagrees with it, the worst he can do is fail me.

—*Junior*

Tested greatly

College is wonderful but different, open, free. Girls, I can't tell you how many things I remember from Bible

Study, even from fifth grade. They are so true. I have been tested greatly thus far, and it is so hard and unbelievable how right, good, and okay things seem. I would be lost and in search of something I could never find if I didn't have Jesus Christ. I never thought that if I actually did seek God first, every single thing, huge or trivial, would fall perfectly into place. I am so thankful! I'm also being exposed to different types of religions and beliefs. There are many variations to Christian beliefs, and I'm watching out for that, too.

—*Freshman*

Makes me want to be more Christian

I'm taking a philosophy class, and today we discussed the problem of evil. The teacher role-played an atheist and argued that God did not exist. It was a heated discussion! I'm kind of mad, though, because it never got resolved (within class). The teacher let us go without really coming to a conclusion, so we'll probably finish it on Thursday. It's incredible though! I mean, if someone believes something they aren't afraid to say it. I really have to know what I believe in that class! It's really interesting, though, and makes me want to be a Christian even more because the ones who aren't, you can tell, are lost and just don't understand. I realize each day more and more how important it is to have a relationship with Jesus. I can't believe how people live without Him.

—*Freshman*

Question everything

Question everything before you believe it. So many things sound good, but in reality, in light, they are totally wrong. I found myself thinking that drugs really aren't that bad the other day after talking to friends. That is crazy. Believe what you believe with all your being or it will waver.

—Sophomore

Learn from people who believe differently

It is difficult, but don't miss new kinds of people just because they don't believe the way you do. Take the time to learn about why they are the way they are. Talk to them and try to understand where they are coming from. Be an example for them of how a Christian should live. Then tell them about yourself and what you believe. People will challenge your beliefs, and you need to not only know what "the rules of being a Christian" are but also why you believe the way you do and also be able to explain it to the people you meet. The wonderful thing is that with every new person you meet, there is the opportunity to learn something from them. College is a time in your life where you will learn the most about yourself and life in general.

—Freshman

Sharing Your Faith

Sharing Your Faith

"What you heard from me, keep as the pattern of sound teaching, with faith and love in Christ Jesus. Guard the good deposit that was entrusted to you—guard it with the help of the Holy Spirit who lives in us." —2 Timothy 1:13–14

"Preach the Word; be prepared in season and out of season." —2 Timothy 4:2

So much of life is caught and not taught. "The way we live either underlines or crosses out everything we say." I saw that quote on a church billboard one day, and it has always stuck with me. College is the perfect place to share your faith. People are searching and don't even know what they are searching for. Be ready to share the hope that you have in Jesus Christ. Pray to win the right to be heard. Live your life in the power of the Holy Spirit, and your friends and acquaintances will wonder what you have—and want it, too!

131

The world needs God

Since I've been thinking so much lately, it has been making me realize just how much God is needed in this world! Through different people and their actions, it all makes me just want to be a servant and live for Him. I try my best, yet it is so hard with all of the sin and pressures always around me. But it is also the greatest opportunity ever! I have so much to be thankful for, and I keep praying everyday that I'll realize it more and more. I know how important it is for Jesus. It makes me want to just tell everyone I can about Him.

—Freshman

I'm going to do something

I've found that I'm just not the way I used to be. Two and a half years of college have taken a toll and worn off on me. I knew that I needed to get back into a Bible study and be with Christian friends. Well, at Christmas three of us went on Christmas Conference with Campus Crusade. It was what I needed for so long. The encouragement and challenge reminded me that our sorority house is not exactly overflowing with bold Christians (or Christians at all!). So God really convicted us of not even letting people know how important He is in our lives. We decided that when we came back to school this semester, we were going to do something—we just didn't know what. The first night back I decided to tell our sorority president about Christmas and our conviction. After I gave her my spiel about wanting to see God work in our house, she looked at me and said, "Well, what are you going to do about it?" That knocked me out of my chair. Here I was just trying to get God wholly in charge of me again, and now I was going to have to "do something" for everyone else! We started a Bible study with freshmen. And I have become so committed to prayer. I can't even begin to tell you what God is doing in this house and on campus. Random friends are asking questions, and I didn't even know that they knew who God was.

—*Junior*

CHAPTER 14

When Life Doesn't Go As Planned

When Life Doesn't Go As Planned

"Praise be to the God and Father of our Lord Jesus Christ, the Father of compassion and the God of all comfort, who comforts us in all our troubles, so that we can comfort those in any trouble with the comfort we ourselves have received from God." —2 Corinthians 1: 3–4

L ife is filled with interruptions, irritations, and changes of plans. Adjustments are made all through our days to compensate for life not going our way. But sometimes an explosion goes off with the destructive power of dynamite. The course we are on is forever altered. Life is never again humdrum, dull, or tediously repetitive. It is now a matter of survival.

Mary Susan Lewis was a beautiful senior at the University of Texas. Coming home from class, she had a seizure caused by a brain tumor that eventually took her life. The night before her surgery, I was with her at the hospital, as her mother needed to be with her dad who was, at that time, dying of brain cancer. She asked me to cut her gorgeous long blonde hair. "Let's see what I would look like with a new hairdo before they shave it off," she remarked. I cut while she ate M&M cookies. Her reflections were written to me on my birthday—just four months before her death.

Carleton Parnell recently lost her life to a rare form of bone cancer. I had the high privilege and blessing of walking beside her during that journey, especially the last five weeks of her life. We shared our combined cancer experiences and had a good time comparing notes. Carleton turned what could have been a disaster into a tremendous adventure. She shared openly and made such a difference in the world of cancer. Carleton was the recipient of the American Cancer Society Life Inspiration Award 2002. Her reflections were written seven months before her death. Carleton knew that this book would be dedicated to her. "Do you want me to read you what I wrote?" I asked her. "No, I want to be surprised!" she replied.

Even in those seemingly dark days, God is there! He cares! He understands! He is the same yesterday, today, and tomorrow. From little problems to gigantic pain—God. From the beginning of college to the end of college—God. From the beginning of life to the end of life—God. He makes no mistakes and is forever holding us in His everlasting arms. In God's economy there are no interruptions—only opportunities. Make the most of every single day!

138

Trying to understand cancer

Until this past December, I thought my life was beginning to have a steady pace. I was starting my junior year at college, had decided to major in graphic design, and was on my way to the big finish line. Even when you think your life is perfect, something can come along so fast and change everything. My life changed on December 29, 2000, when I was diagnosed with cancer. After I left the doctor's office, did all the crying I could do, and asked all the questions I could ask, I knew I had to make the best of this awful situation because cancer is something a person cannot run from. I gathered all my friends and told my story. I'll never forget the look in their eyes. They had no idea what to say or how to act. I was about to go through something we thought none of us would ever have to deal with at the age of 21. The only words I could think of to comfort them were, "I am strong and patient, and only God can heal me."

My whole outlook on life has changed since my one-year experience with cancer. I used to wake up every day and grudgingly get out of bed, but now I feel blessed to wake up. I always said yes to everything; now that I have limitations, I wonder why I said yes to so many past actions that got me in trouble. I used to think I was a mature adult, but looking back I see that I wasn't. I took for granted the positive aspects I had in my life, till now.

The hardest thing I face is the way other people make me feel uncomfortable. True friends stick out. I am the first person in my graduating high school class to be diagnosed with cancer. Many of my classmates are able to put aside everything and see me for who I am. My parents' friends have given me the gift of love. Last year, if I had heard of a friend with an illness, I would have thought of writing them a note but never have followed through. The letters I've received have shown me the true meaning of life, love, and the way to brighten a person's heart

I've often wondered about the meaning of being diagnosed with cancer. Who is chosen and who is excluded? I believe that God has many obstacles in store for everyone, some being harder than others. I hope that someday, looking back, I will learn a little more about this obstacle from God.

—*Carleton Parnell, Senior*

Testimony

I delivered my testimony at a student meeting last week, and I quoted you in it. I remember you saying, "It was only natural for me to give my difficult circumstances to God, because I had been in the habit of giving things up to God every day long before I knew the storms He had planned for me." But as the opportunity to present my testimony challenged me to glance back and isolate the remarkable points in my new life in Jesus, I realized you have made more of an impact on my life that I give you credit for. You were the first person who really challenged me to study the Bible, the first person who ever suggested that I spend a quiet time with the Lord, and the first and *only* person to take me to Six Flags, Lenox Square, Rock City, and the Chattanooga Choo Choo for memorizing Scripture. You provided a fun environment for me to meet other girls my age and to bring my friends, too. And then, there you were—M&M cookies in hand—when I made my unexpected visit to Birmingham. Thanks, Donna. I love you and appreciate you. You've been to me a teacher, a role model, a discipler, and a friend.

—Mary Susan Lewis, Senior

When friends like the same guy

Often in the college setting, many girls end up liking the same guy. When two girls like the same guy, emotions get high. What can be done to soften hearts and save friendships? We don't own anyone. Oftentimes the process of holding your hands open is very difficult. In fact, for me it's impossible apart from God.

My advice as you prepare for college is this: remember that life is filled with change. Many life lessons are learned through relationships. Hold all people loosely and trust God to give or take according to His plan. If you are in a relationship with a guy, be thankful and please God with your actions. You will probably date a lot of people during your college years. Be open, honest, moral, forgiving, and accepting. Be certain this will save a lot of confusion. Remember at times you will be hurt, but also remember that you will hurt others as well. Keep short accounts.

—Sophomore

A desperate prayer

Holy Father, I need Your help. I am so alone and far from You. I have not been living for You and I am to the point where I can't help myself. Please take over. Redeem me, Father. Carry me through the lonely times and hold me tight. Let me rest in You because I am weary. I don't even know what to do next, so please send Your Holy Spirit to guide me and be my comforter. Lead me to new friends who love You. Help me to find a body of believers who can strengthen me. You have never broken a promise, so I believe Your promise that You would never abandon or forsake me. So please remember the little girl who gave You her heart so long ago. I am desperate. Please don't delay!

—Sophomore

A thankful prayer

Holy Father, You are so good to me! I am forever undeserving and have done countless bad things, but Your love and mercy covers all of them. You have restored to me the joy of my salvation. My heart overflows with thankfulness for You pulling me out of the pit I created for myself. It amazes me that even though I walked in such dark places, You were with me and forgive me. You truly forgive me. As I look back from where You brought me, please protect me from the enemy. Don't let him steal my joy again. Thank You for showing me that the things of the past are exactly that: the things of the past. I am a new creation and beautiful in Your sight. I am grateful that I traded my heavy robe of guilt for a garment of salvation and praise.

I thank You for Your perfect plan for my life. Use my past experiences to glorify You in some way. That is what You do: bring good out of evil and new life from death. So as You turn my rags to splendor, help me to be on guard, stand firm in the faith You give me, be strong and courageous, and do everything in love.

Oh, Lord, as Your beauty reflects from me, I am forever thankful that You have called even me to be the aroma of Christ. I love You so much.

—*Senior*

My plan, God's plan

I was going to be your typical four-year college student. I would take at least 15 hours a semester, immediately choose my major, and pursue an education with a career in mind. That was *my* plan; but God's plan doesn't always go according to our expectations. I was making good grades, forming new friendships, and I had found a church; my plan was falling into place, but in November of my freshman year, I got sick and spent a week in the hospital. I was able to recover and finish the year. Well, the first semester of my sophomore year, I was forced to withdraw from school once again due to illness.

Looking back, I might wish parts of God's plan had been different, but I wouldn't change anything. I believe it would have been easier for me to handle the interruptions had I not expected so much; I now remind myself to "accept, not expect." Hardships in our lives aren't sent by God, but He allows them to happen, and He cries with us, laughs with us, and hurts with us. We have the comfort of knowing that God is always in control and is constantly working for the good. We don't see the positive side of upsetting events until God is ready for us to see them. When we pray and pray and things don't go our way, it has nothing to do with God not listening; this is usually an indicator that His plan is in progress. When life doesn't go according to your wishes, take that as a sign that God is working. Enjoy the road ahead, and don't forget to let God be the driver.

—Sophomore

God loves you unconditionally

My advice to you girls is to walk closely with Jesus from the day you set foot on campus. Put Him first and your life will be joyful. But if you do have regrets, remember that He loves you unconditionally. There is nothing you can do to make Him love you any more or any less. College is a great experience. Make the most of it and invest all for eternity.

—*Senior*

Girls whose letters were quoted

Murray Abernethy—Washington and Lee University
Kate Adams—University of Mississippi
Katherine Alford—University of Virginia
Laura Ann Baker—Auburn University
Katie Baldwin—Washington and Lee University
Michelle Bargeron—Vanderbilt University
Miller Beale—Princeton University
Betsy Blan—Furman University
Lauren Britton—University of Georgia
Whitney Brockman—University of Colorado
Robyn Caldwell—University of Alabama
Courtney Carlisle—Furman University
Maggie Carter—Auburn University
Jane Chambliss—University of Mississippi
Melissa Craig—University of Mississippi
Ashley Davenport—Birmingham Southern College
Emily deFuniak—University of Mississippi
Elizabeth Drennen—Hollins University
Kat Drennen—Hollins University
Mary Drennen—Washington and Lee University
Elizabeth Fendley—Furman University
Amy Fitzgerald—Auburn University
Laura Glenn—University of Mississippi
Susan Graham—Auburn University
Christine Grayson—Southern Methodist University

Bradford Greene—Auburn University

Kimberly Guy—Auburn University

Virginia Hanson—University of North Carolina, Chapel Hill

Maye Head—Yale University

Mary Margaret Hiller—Auburn University

Rebecca Hiller—Auburn University

Katherine Jackson—Wheaton College

Erin Kattus—Auburn University

Mary Susan Lewis—University of Texas

Courtney Lukens—Auburn University

Karen Lytle—Davidson College

Claire Magnus—Auburn University

Ellen Magnus—Auburn University

Eliza Martin—Vanderbilt University

Maggie McDonald—Rhodes College

Rachel McIntosh—Auburn University

Rushton Mellen—Auburn University

Marlowe Mitchell—Northwestern University

Brooke Moor—University of Alabama

Jordan Orso—Auburn University

Meg Paine—University of Mississippi

Allene Parnell—University of Georgia

Carleton Parnell—University of Alabama

Carrie Pittman—Southern Methodist University

Leslie Pittman—Southern Methodist University

Emily Putnam—Auburn University

Celeste Raburn—University of Alabama

Sally Richardson—Hollins University

Katie Rooney—University of Virginia
Katie Sandlin—Auburn University
Jane Kathryn Saunders—University of Mississippi
Lindsey Smith—Vanderbilt University
Christian Stevens—Washington and Lee University
Kate Stutts—University of Mississippi
Thames Thuston—University of Virginia
Sarah Torsch—Auburn University
Eleanor Twiford—University of Mississippi
Jeanne Upchurch—Washington and Lee University
Kit Upchurch—Presbyterian College
Shannon Upchurch—Washington and Lee University
Corinne Vann—University of Georgia
Forrest Walker—University of Alabama
Lauren Watkins—Vanderbilt University
Christy White—University of Tennessee
Martha Jane Wood—University of Mississippi
Whitney Wright—Southern Methodist University
Gail Harper Yeilding—Boston College
Ruth Hill Yeilding—Washington and Lee University

Colleges and universities represented

Auburn University

Birmingham-Southern College

Boston College

Davidson College

Furman University

Hollins University

Northwestern University

Presbyterian College

Princeton University

Rhodes College

Samford University

Southern Methodist University

University of Alabama

University of Colorado

University of Georgia

University of Mississippi (Ole Miss)

University of North Carolina (Chapel Hill)

University of Tennessee

University of Texas

University of Virginia

Vanderbilt University

Washington and Lee University

Wheaton College

Yale University